PRESENTATION

INTRODUCTION TO THE VALUATION OF HUMAN CAPITAL

WISDOM OF EXPERIENCE

EVALUATING INTERNAL COMPETENCIES

CONTINUOUS TALENT DEVELOPMENT

BUILDING INTERNAL LEADERSHIP

THE COST OF TURNOVER

INTEGRATION AND MENTORING

RECOGNITION AND REWARD

TWO-DIRECTIONAL FEEDBACK

TAKE ADVANTAGE OF AGE DIVERSITY

THE POWER OF INTERNAL NETWORKS

REDEFINING INDOOR MOBILITY

PREVENTING SKILLS OBSOLESCENCE

ORGANIZATIONAL CULTURE AND RETENTION

PERFORMANCE ASSESSMENT TOOLS

BALANCE BETWEEN NEW AND OLD

TRAINING AND DEVELOPMENT

SUCCESSION PLANS

ENCOURAGING INTERNAL INNOVATION

CHANGE MANAGEMENT

CREATIVE SOLUTIONS TO BUSINESS CHALLENGES

THE IMPACT OF EMPLOYEE SATISFACTION

CREATING A BUSINESS LEGACY

THE FUTURE OF TALENT MANAGEMENT

REGINALDO OSNILDO

Valuing experience: the strength of internal skills and the importance of retaining talent

Copyright © 2024 Reginaldo Osnildo
All rights reserved.

PRESENTATION

Welcome to the beginning of a transformative journey within the universe of management and business leadership with the book **" Valuing experience: the strength of internal skills and the importance of retaining talent"** . By choosing this guide, you are preparing to dive into deep insights and practical strategies that will revolutionize the way you view and manage human capital in your organization.

This book has been carefully crafted for leaders and managers, like you, who recognize the invaluable value of long-term employees and want to tap into internal competencies for mutual benefit. Here, you'll find a compilation of inspiring examples and proven techniques to strengthen company culture, improve talent retention, and drive your business success by investing in the people who are the true essence of your company.

Each chapter in this book is designed to be complete in itself, but also as part of a cohesive whole that builds a broad and integrated understanding of valuing internal talents. From introducing basic concepts about the importance of valuing human capital to advanced strategies for change management and internal innovation, this book serves as a roadmap for navigating the challenges and opportunities of retaining and developing experienced employees.

By adapting and updating classic concepts with a new vision, this book not only synthesizes essential knowledge but also introduces my modernized insights and approaches that are directly applicable to today's corporate environment. Prepared to be as practical as it is inspiring, it is the ideal resource for you who seek not only to understand, but to effectively apply the art of valuing and retaining talent within your organization.

I now invite you to turn the page and start with our **INTRODUCTION TO THE VALUATION OF HUMAN CAPITAL**, where we will explore how valuing your employees can transform your company from the inside out. This first step will help you understand the basis of everything we will discuss later, setting the tone for learning that will be as rewarding as it is essential.

Prepare yourself for a read that promises to not only inform, but also inspire and equip you with everything you need to make a real and lasting difference in your organization. Let's go together on this journey of discovery and transformation. Advance to the next chapter and start shaping the future of talent management at your company.

Yours sincerely

Reginaldo Osnildo

INTRODUCTION TO THE VALUATION OF HUMAN CAPITAL

By embarking on this journey, you are taking the first step towards a profound transformation in the way your company values its most dedicated employees. This opening chapter offers a comprehensive overview of the meaning and importance of recognizing and valuing human capital, especially those who dedicate years of service and effort to the growth of their organization.

THE BASIS OF EVERYTHING: WHAT IS HUMAN CAPITAL?

Human capital refers to the set of skills, knowledge and experience that employees bring to your organization. This is the engine that drives innovation, productivity and, ultimately, success in today's competitive marketplace. Valuing this capital means recognizing and investing in the people who dedicate their careers to the advancement of your company. It is an investment that brings multiplied returns, not only in terms of financial results, but also in the enrichment of corporate culture and general employee satisfaction.

WHY VALUE LONG-TERM EMPLOYEES?

Long-time employees are treasures of knowledge and experience. They not only understand the ins and outs of the company but also form the backbone of your organizational culture. Valuing these employees demonstrates a commitment to stability and continuous growth, sending a powerful message to the entire team: here, loyalty and effort are recognized and rewarded.

THE BENEFITS OF INVESTING IN EXPERIENCE

1. **Talent retention:** Employees who feel valued tend to remain with the company. This reduces hiring and training costs and ensures critical knowledge is maintained within the organization.
2. **Increased productivity:** With high morale, there is a natural increase in productivity. Happy and engaged employees contribute more and better.

3. **Innovation from experience:** Contrary to popular belief, long-time employees can be great innovators. With the right support, they use their experience to shape innovative solutions that newcomers might not be able to envision.
4. **Promotion of corporate culture:** Veteran employees help to perpetuate and strengthen the company's culture and values, acting as mentors for younger employees and ensuring the continuity of organizational standards and ethics.

HOW CAN YOU START?

Valuing human capital begins with recognizing individual contributions and understanding that each employee is unique. Recognition initiatives, personalized development programs and growth opportunities tailored to individual needs and career goals are essential.

This chapter only offers an overview of the importance of valuing human capital. In the next chapters, you will discover concrete, detailed strategies for cultivating and maintaining this valuable resource. From now on, every step you take with this book will open new doors to transform your organization in meaningful and lasting ways.

Get ready to explore the **WISDOM OF EXPERIENCE** in the next chapter, where we take a deep dive into the ways in which accumulated experience can be a powerful lever for business success. You will learn how experience not only sustains but also drives efficiency and innovation in your organization. Let's uncover these secrets together and ensure your company not only survives, but thrives by recognizing the true strength that resides in your most experienced employees.

WISDOM OF EXPERIENCE

Now that we understand the crucial importance of valuing human capital, let's dive deeper into the " **WISDOM OF EXPERIENCE** " in this chapter. Long-time employees are not just witnesses to your company's history; They are also holders of insights, skills and knowledge that only time can provide. Here, we will explore how this accumulated experience is an invaluable asset that strengthens organizational culture and increases operational efficiency, benefiting the entire company.

EXPERIENCE AS A PILLAR OF ORGANIZATIONAL CULTURE

Experienced employees are more than just workers; they are the guardians of your company's culture and traditions. With years, sometimes decades, of service, these individuals have an intimate understanding of the values and practices that define their organization. They play a crucial role in orienting new employees, not only teaching them the ropes from a technical standpoint but also immersing them in the cultural aspects that make your company unique.

OPERATIONAL EFFICIENCY DRIVED BY EXPERIENCE

Long-term employees have an operational efficiency that only comes with time. They know the nuances of their roles and are often able to identify and resolve problems long before they become critical. This skill not only saves time and resources, but also serves as an excellent example for younger colleagues who are still learning to navigate their own roles.

THE POWER OF MENTORING

One of the biggest benefits of retaining experienced employees is their ability to act as mentors. Mentoring goes beyond training; it is a transfer of wisdom, offering guidance and advice that can only be given by someone who has lived many experiences. This mentoring relationship strengthens teams, creates a more cohesive work environment, and helps ensure that the company's legacy continues to thrive with new generations.

CHALLENGES AND OPPORTUNITIES

However, employing and engaging long-term employees also presents challenges. How can you, as a manager or leader, ensure that they feel valued and motivated to continue actively contributing? It is crucial to recognize that experience does not equate to stagnation. Investing in the continuous development of these employees, providing them with new opportunities for learning and growth, is essential to maintain their motivation and satisfaction at work.

STRATEGIES TO CAPITALIZE ON EXPERIENCE

1. **Creation of internal consultancy panels:** Use the experience of your older employees by forming panels that can offer insights into strategic decisions.
2. **Knowledge exchange programs:** Encourage knowledge exchange between employees of different generations and departments to increase innovation and mutual learning.
3. **Process review:** Employ the experience of your veterans to review and improve internal processes, maximizing operational efficiency.

By valuing and appropriately employing the wisdom of your most experienced employees, you not only improve the effectiveness of your operations, but also strengthen the organizational culture, create a solid foundation for the future, and foster an environment where everyone feels an integral part of the company's success. company.

As we move to the next chapter, " **EVALUATING INTERNAL COMPETENCIES**," you will learn methods for identifying untapped skills and talents within your team. This is an opportunity to discover how to further harness the potential of all your employees, expanding the benefits of accumulated experience and integrating it with new capabilities and visions.

EVALUATING INTERNAL COMPETENCIES

You have already discovered the importance of valuing accumulated experience and how it strengthens your company's culture and operational efficiency. Now, in the chapter "**EVALUATING INTERNAL COMPETENCIES**", we will explore practical methods for identifying untapped skills, talents and competencies within your team. This assessment is essential for fully utilizing the potential of your employees and for creating a truly adaptive and resilient organization.

UNDERSTANDING INTERNAL COMPETENCIES

An organization's internal competencies include all the skills, knowledge and capabilities that employees possess, many of which may not be fully utilized. The challenge is to discover these hidden skills and understand how they can be mobilized to strengthen the company and drive innovation.

METHODS FOR IDENTIFYING COMPETENCIES

1. **Performance reviews:** Use regular reviews to not only review performance, but also to identify underutilized or developing skills that may be crucial for future projects or positions.
2. **Skills surveys:** Implement surveys that allow employees to report skills and interests that are not applicable in their current roles. This can reveal hidden talents that could benefit the company in innovative ways.
3. **Focus groups and workshops:** Organize sessions where employees can discuss their experiences and aspirations. These meetings are opportunities to discover skills that are not visible in everyday life.
4. **Internal network analysis:** Use network analysis to see how employees collaborate with each other. This can help identify informal leaders and experts on specific topics who could be better leveraged.

INTEGRATING COMPETENCIES INTO ORGANIZATIONAL

STRATEGY

Once identified, internal competencies must be integrated strategically. This can be done through:

- **Role redesign:** Adapt existing roles to better utilize identified skills, allowing employees to contribute more meaningfully.
- **Formation of project teams:** Create multidisciplinary teams for specific projects that use a variety of internal skills, promoting innovation and mutual learning.
- **Development programs:** Provide targeted training and development to enhance existing competencies and develop new skills that benefit both individuals and the organization.

CHALLENGES IN SKILLS ASSESSMENT

Assessing internal competencies can face resistance, especially if employees feel it could threaten their current roles. It is vital to approach these initiatives with transparency, clearly communicating how skills assessment is an opportunity for everyone's personal and professional growth.

This chapter has equipped you with tools to begin discovering and leveraging your team's internal competencies. As a leader or manager, you have the opportunity to transform this information into actions that not only maximize the potential of your employees, but also propel your organization to new levels of success.

In the next chapter, " **CONTINUOUS TALENT DEVELOPMENT** ", we will cover strategies to foster employees' professional and personal growth. We will continue to explore how to keep employees engaged and motivated, making the most of the vast pool of talent within your organization.

CONTINUOUS TALENT DEVELOPMENT

Having explored how to identify your team's internal competencies, we now turn to one of the most vital pillars for sustaining a dynamic and adaptive organization: continuous talent development. This chapter is intended to offer you, the leader or manager, practical strategies to foster not only the professional growth, but also the personal growth of your employees, keeping them engaged and motivated.

THE IMPORTANCE OF CONTINUOUS DEVELOPMENT

Employees who perceive opportunities for continuous growth tend to be more engaged and productive. Continuous talent development doesn't just benefit individuals; it enriches the entire organization by cultivating a continuous learning environment that encourages innovation and adaptability.

STRATEGIES TO FOSTER GROWTH

1. **Individualized development plans:** Create development plans that are personalized to each employee's needs and career aspirations. This shows a genuine investment in your future within the company.
2. **Mentoring and coaching:** Establish mentoring programs where more experienced employees can guide younger ones. Coaching by external professionals can also be an excellent tool for developing specific skills.
3. **Ongoing training and education:** Offer regular access to courses, workshops and seminars that can help employees update and expand their skills.
4. **Challenging projects:** Assign projects that challenge employees to step out of their comfort zones and apply their skills in new and innovative ways.
5. **Continuous feedback:** Implement a feedback system that not only evaluates performance, but also offers guidance and support for personal and professional growth.

OVERCOMING OBSTACLES TO DEVELOPMENT

Addressing barriers to ongoing talent development is crucial. These obstacles can include lack of time, limited resources, or even a company culture that doesn't value continuous learning. Overcoming them may require a change of mindset in leadership and a commitment to investing in human capital as a strategic priority.

EVALUATING DEVELOPMENT SUCCESS

The success of your talent development efforts can be measured through several metrics, such as increased job satisfaction, better performance on performance reviews, and lower employee turnover. Maintaining a robust evaluation system will help ensure that investment in talent development is truly benefiting both individuals and the organization as a whole.

This chapter has provided the tools and knowledge you need to implement and sustain a culture of continuous talent development. By doing so, you will not only increase employee satisfaction and retention, but you will also strengthen your company's foundation for future success.

In the next chapter, " **BUILDING INTERNAL LEADERSHIP** ", we will explore the importance of cultivating leaders within the organization itself and how this can encourage loyalty and dedication, as well as reinforce corporate governance and strategy. Advance through the book and discover how to transform potential into effective leadership, and how these leaders can help lead your organization to new heights of success.

BUILDING INTERNAL LEADERSHIP

As we move forward on our journey to strengthen talent management practices within your organization, it is crucial that we focus on building and promoting internal leadership. This chapter addresses the importance of cultivating leaders within your own company and how this can not only encourage loyalty and dedication, but also reinforce organizational structure and effectiveness as a whole.

THE IMPORTANCE OF INTERNAL LEADERSHIP

Developing internal leaders is a vital strategy for the long-term sustainability of any organization. Leaders who grow within the company have a deep understanding of its culture, processes and challenges. They are therefore in a unique position to shape the future of the organization in a way that is aligned with its values and vision.

STRATEGIES TO FOSTER INTERNAL LEADERSHIP

1. **Identifying potential leaders:** Use performance assessments and ongoing feedback to identify employees who have leadership potential. Special attention should be paid not only to technical skills, but also to interpersonal and management skills.
2. **Leadership development programs:** Implement specific training programs to develop necessary leadership skills. This can include workshops, seminars, coaching, and even rotational leadership experiences.
3. **Hands-on leadership opportunities:** Offer potential leaders opportunities to lead projects or teams, even in a temporary context. This practical experience is invaluable for developing leadership skills.
4. **Executive Mentoring:** Connect emerging leaders with executives and senior managers through mentoring programs. This not only helps with skill development, but also facilitates tacit knowledge transfer and cultural integration.

BENEFITS OF INTERNAL LEADERSHIP

- **Better talent retention:** Leaders who are promoted from within are more likely to stay with the company, reducing costs associated with turnover and recruitment.
- **Cultural alignment:** Internal leaders are ambassadors of the company's culture, ensuring that decisions and innovations are aligned with organizational values.
- **Continuity and stability:** Promoting leaders from within ensures a smoother transition with less disruption to day-to-day operations.

CHALLENGES IN BUILDING INTERNAL LEADERSHIP

Building internal leadership is not without its challenges. Issues such as resistance to change, insecurity among peers and the need for substantial investments in development may arise. Overcoming these challenges requires effective communication, a clear career development policy and a commitment to employees' personal and professional growth.

This chapter outlined the essential strategy for building leadership within your organization. By investing in the growth of your leaders, you are not only enhancing individual capabilities but also strengthening your company's foundation for the future.

In the next chapter, " **THE COST OF TURNOVER** ," we will explore the financial and cultural impacts of high employee turnover and how effective retention strategies, including valuing and developing internal talent, can significantly reduce these costs.

THE COST OF TURNOVER

In the previous chapter, we explored how building internal leadership can enrich your organization. Now, let's look at a significant challenge faced by many companies: high employee turnover. This chapter will discuss the financial and cultural impacts of high turnover and how effective retention strategies can not only minimize these costs but also strengthen the corporate environment.

UNDERSTANDING TURNOVER

Turnover, or employee turnover, refers to the process by which employees leave the company and are replaced by new ones. While some degree of turnover is normal and even healthy for bringing in new ideas and skills, a high rate may be symptomatic of deeper problems within the organization, including job dissatisfaction, lack of growth opportunities or management failures.

FINANCIAL IMPACTS OF TURNOVER

The costs associated with employee turnover are often underestimated. They include:

1. **Recruitment and training costs:** Searching, hiring and training new employees takes considerable time and resources.
2. **Loss of productivity:** New employees often take time to reach the productivity level of their predecessors.
3. **Separation costs:** Depending on local laws and company policies, there may be significant termination costs.

CULTURAL IMPACTS OF TURNOVER

In addition to tangible costs, high turnover can have a profound impact on company culture:

- **Loss of knowledge:** When experienced employees leave, they take valuable institutional knowledge with them.
- **Decreased engagement:** High turnover can affect the morale of remaining employees, who may feel insecure

about their own positions or demotivated by the unstable environment.
- **Difficulties in transmitting culture:** Long-time employees play a crucial role in instilling the company's values and practices to newcomers. High turnover can make it difficult to maintain organizational culture.

STRATEGIES TO REDUCE TURNOVER

1. **Improving job satisfaction:** Investing in the work environment, ensuring that employees feel valued, understood and part of something bigger.
2. **Career development and progression:** Provide clear career paths and development opportunities to encourage employees to grow within the company.
3. **Effective feedback and communication:** Maintain open lines of communication and offer regular feedback to help employees understand how they contribute to company goals.

This chapter has highlighted the significant cost associated with high turnover and how strategic retention approaches can turn this challenge into an opportunity to strengthen the workforce and company culture. By implementing the strategies discussed, you can reduce turnover and create an environment where employees not only want to stay, but thrive.

In the next chapter, " **INTEGRATION AND MENTORING** ", we will explore how the experience of established employees can be used to mentor new employees, facilitating integration and strengthening organizational culture.

INTEGRATION AND MENTORING

After discussing the importance of minimizing turnover and its implications in the previous chapter, we will now explore effective onboarding and mentoring strategies. This chapter will highlight how the knowledge and experience of established employees can be essential not only for mentoring new employees, but also for strengthening organizational culture and promoting smooth integration that benefits the entire company.

THE IMPORTANCE OF EFFECTIVE INTEGRATION

The integration, or onboarding, of new employees is a crucial process for the long-term success of both the employee and the organization. Effective onboarding goes beyond simple technical training; it includes immersion in the company's culture, values and expectations, ensuring that new members feel welcome and prepared for their new roles.

THE ROLE OF MENTORING

Mentoring is a powerful tool that links individual development to organizational success. Through mentoring, more experienced employees share their knowledge and experience, helping newcomers navigate the early challenges of their careers at the company and accelerating their professional development.

STRATEGIES FOR IMPLEMENTING EFFECTIVE MENTORING PROGRAMS

1. **Conscious pairing:** Mentors should be chosen not only for their technical expertise, but also for their interpersonal skills and commitment to developing others. Pairing should consider the personality and career goals of mentors and mentees.
2. **Setting clear goals:** Both the mentor and mentee should have a clear understanding of the mentoring goals, which may include developing specific skills, integrating into the company culture, or enhancing leadership skills.

3. **Organizational support:** Mentoring must be supported by company leadership, with adequate resources and recognition of the time and effort invested by mentors.
4. **Assessment and feedback:** Mentoring programs should include regular feedback and assessment mechanisms, allowing for adjustments as needed to maximize their impact.

BENEFITS OF INTEGRATION AND MENTORING

- **Reduction in turnover:** Employees who go through a well-structured integration process and who receive adequate mentoring are more likely to stay with the company.
- **Accelerated development:** Guidance from a mentor can significantly accelerate a new employee's professional development.
- **Strengthening organizational culture:** Mentoring helps to transmit and reinforce the company's cultural values and norms, promoting a more cohesive and aligned workforce.

Effectively implementing onboarding and mentoring strategies can transform the way new employees are absorbed and developed within your organization. These practices not only improve the employee experience, but also strengthen the company's organizational and cultural structure.

In the next chapter, " **RECOGNITION AND REWARD** ", we'll explore how to create reward systems that value employees' long-term contributions and how this can positively impact motivation and engagement.

RECOGNITION AND REWARD

As we move forward on this journey to strengthen talent management in your organization, it is essential to address the importance of recognition and reward. This chapter discusses how well-structured reward systems not only encourage performance but also promote employee loyalty and satisfaction. By valuing long-term contributions, you foster a motivating and rewarding work environment.

THE IMPORTANCE OF RECOGNIZING AND REWARDING

Employees who feel recognized demonstrate greater job satisfaction and commitment to the company. Recognition is not just a motivation tool; it also strengthens organizational culture, promotes employee loyalty, and encourages behaviors that lead to collective success.

ELEMENTS OF AN EFFECTIVE REWARDS SYSTEM

1. **Fairness and transparency:** Reward policies must be clear, fair and applied consistently. Equity in treatment is essential to avoid perceptions of favoritism, which can be detrimental to team morale.
2. **Diversity of rewards:** Rewards do not need to be exclusively monetary. Public recognition, professional development opportunities, awards and work flexibility are examples of rewards that can be highly valued.
3. **Alignment with organizational objectives:** Rewards must be aligned with the company's long-term objectives and corporate values, encouraging behaviors that contribute to organizational success.
4. **Personalization:** Consider individual preferences when developing reward systems, as what motivates one employee may not be as effective for another.

STRATEGIES FOR IMPLEMENTATION

1. **Formal and informal recognition programs :** Establish programs that recognize both significant achievements

and everyday contributions. This may include annual awards ceremonies and more frequent recognition at team meetings.
2. **Points system:** Implement a points system that allows employees to accumulate rewards based on their performance, which can be exchanged for prizes or benefits.
3. **Continuous feedback:** Combine rewards with regular feedback, ensuring employees understand how their actions contribute to company goals and how they are valued.

BENEFITS OF A ROBUST RECOGNITION SYSTEM

- **Increased motivation and productivity:** Employees who feel valued tend to work harder and more creatively.
- **Talent retention:** Effective reward systems reduce turnover, as employees are more satisfied and engaged.
- **Positive culture:** An environment where recognition is a common practice promotes positivity and collaboration among employees.

Implementing an effective recognition and reward system is crucial to any talent management strategy. These systems not only increase satisfaction and engagement, but also align employees' efforts with the company's larger goals.

In the next chapter, " **TWO-DIRECTIONAL FEEDBACK** ," we will explore the importance of cultivating an environment where feedback is not only given, but also actively solicited from employees. This process strengthens relationships, communication and organizational effectiveness.

TWO-DIRECTIONAL FEEDBACK

After discussing the importance of recognition and reward, we now move on to exploring the power of two-way feedback. This chapter will highlight how to cultivate an environment where feedback is not just delivered, but actively solicited from employees, contributing to the continuous improvement of the organization and building stronger, more transparent relationships between all hierarchical levels.

THE IMPORTANCE OF BIDIRECTIONAL FEEDBACK

Two-way feedback is a vital tool for personal and professional development, as well as organizational health. It allows both managers and employees to share perspectives, increasing mutual understanding and identifying areas for improvement. This process is essential for adapting work practices, aligning expectations and fostering an environment of respect and collaboration.

STRUCTURING BIDIRECTIONAL FEEDBACK

1. **Setting clear expectations:** It is crucial that everyone involved understands the purpose of the feedback, the rules of engagement and how the information will be used.
2. **Creating safe spaces:** Ensure that feedback spaces are perceived as safe and confidential, where employees can express themselves freely without fear of negative repercussions.
3. **Regularity and routine:** Feedback should be an ongoing practice, not limited to annual reviews. Regular meetings and progress reviews can help keep the dialogue open and constructive.
4. **Effective communication training:** Train leaders and employees in communication skills, especially how to give and receive feedback in a constructive way.

BENEFITS OF TWO-DIRECTIONAL FEEDBACK

- **Continuous improvement:** Bottom-up feedback allows leaders to better understand the challenges facing their teams and adjust policies and practices according to real needs.
- **Engagement and motivation:** Employees who feel their voice is heard tend to be more engaged and motivated.
- **Trust and transparency:** Regularly practicing two-way feedback builds trust and promotes a culture of transparency and honesty.

CHALLENGES OF TWO-DIRECTIONAL FEEDBACK

Implementing effective two-way feedback can face obstacles such as cultural resistance to criticism, especially in more hierarchical or traditional organizations. Additionally, a lack of communication skills can distort the intent and content of feedback, leading to misunderstandings and frustration.

This chapter has provided insight into how two-way feedback can be implemented and the benefits it brings to organizational dynamics. By adopting these practices, your company not only improves in efficiency and effectiveness, but also becomes a place where everyone feels valued and an integral part of the collective success.

In the next chapter, " **TAKE ADVANTAGE OF AGE DIVERSITY** ", we will explore how integrating different generations in the workplace can enrich your company, foster innovation and mutual learning

TAKE ADVANTAGE
OF AGE DIVERSITY

Continuing our discussion on innovative talent management practices, we will now address the valuable age diversity in the workplace. This chapter explores how mixing generations can not only enrich your company, but also foster innovation and mutual learning, creating a more dynamic and adaptable environment.

UNDERSTANDING AGE DIVERSITY

Age diversity in the workplace refers to the inclusion of employees of various age groups, from young professionals to seasoned veterans. This diversity brings a wealth of perspectives and experiences that can contribute to organizational growth and innovation.

BENEFITS OF AGE DIVERSITY

1. **Increased innovation:** Combining new ideas and life experiences can lead to innovative solutions that would not be possible in a homogeneous group.
2. **Knowledge transfer:** More experienced employees can share crucial knowledge with younger colleagues, while the latter can bring technological skills and current trends to the team.
3. **Organizational flexibility and resilience:** Age-diverse teams are often more flexible and adaptable to change, as they combine the wisdom of experience with the adaptability of youth.

STRATEGIES FOR CULTIVATING AGE DIVERSITY

1. **Inclusive recruitment policies:** Ensure that recruitment processes are not biased towards certain age groups, promoting equal opportunities for all candidates.
2. **programs :** Implement mentoring programs where youth and veterans can learn from each other, leveraging the strengths of each generation.
3. **Continuing professional development:** Provide

development opportunities that meet career needs at different life stages, encouraging continued growth and job satisfaction.
4. **Creating multigenerational teams:** Form teams that include members of various ages for specific projects, promoting intergenerational collaboration.

CHALLENGES OF AGE DIVERSITY

While age diversity offers many benefits, it can also present challenges, such as communication differences and value conflicts between generations. Overcoming these challenges requires a commitment to training and practices that promote respect and mutual understanding.

This chapter has highlighted how age diversity can be a source of strength and innovation for your company. By adopting strategies that promote an inclusive and collaborative work environment, you can maximize the potential of all employees, regardless of their age.

In the next chapter, " **THE POWER OF INTERNAL NETWORKS** ," we'll explore how to value and cultivate the connections that employees build inside and outside the company. Read on and discover how these internal networks can be capitalized on to further strengthen your organization.

THE POWER OF INTERNAL NETWORKS

As we continue exploring ways to strengthen your organization, in this chapter we will cover the " **POWER OF INTERNAL NETWORKS** ." Let's investigate how the connections that employees make inside and outside the company can be a valuable resource for organizational growth and innovation.

UNDERSTANDING INTERNAL NETWORKS

Internal networks refer to the fabric of relationships that employees develop with each other within an organization. These networks include formal connections, such as project teams, and informal ones, such as friendships and collaborative partnerships. The strength of these networks is crucial for information dissemination, effective collaboration, and mutual support.

BENEFITS OF INTERNAL NETWORKS

1. **Improved communication and collaboration:** Strong networks facilitate efficient communication and sharing of ideas, which can accelerate innovation and problem solving.
2. **Knowledge management support:** Robust internal connections help ensure that valuable knowledge is shared and not lost when employees leave.
3. **Strengthening organizational culture:** Well-developed internal networks promote a sense of community and belonging, which can increase job satisfaction and employee retention.

STRATEGIES FOR CULTIVATING STRONG INTERNAL NETWORKS

1. **Promoting networking events:** Host regular events that encourage employees to connect with each other in an informal setting. This may include networking meetings, team lunches and team building activities.
2. **Use of collaboration technology:** Implement collaboration tools that facilitate real-time

communication and information sharing , especially useful for connecting remote or geographically dispersed teams.
3. **Mentoring and mentoring programs:** Encourage the formation of networks through mentoring programs that connect employees from different levels and departments.
4. **Special interest groups:** Support the creation of special interest groups within the organization, which can help cultivate networks around common hobbies or shared professional goals.

CHALLENGES IN CULTIVATING INTERNAL NETWORKS

Despite its many benefits, developing effective internal networks can be challenging due to resistance to change, a lack of employee engagement, or an organizational culture that does not promote interaction. Overcoming these challenges requires committed leadership and the implementation of policies that promote and value the building of networks.

This chapter has highlighted the significant value of internal networks and how they can be strategically cultivated to benefit your organization. By investing in the development of these networks, you are strengthening not only daily operations but also long-term organizational resilience.

In the next chapter, " **REDEFINING INDOOR MOBILITY**", we'll explore how facilitating internal mobility can allow your employees to explore new areas within the company, promoting talent retention and development.

REDEFINING INDOOR MOBILITY

In this chapter, we will focus on " **REDEFINING INDOOR MOBILITY**", a key strategy for keeping your organization dynamic and adaptable by allowing employees to explore new areas within the company. Internal mobility not only promotes talent retention and development, but also enriches the employee experience, keeping them motivated and engaged.

WHAT IS INTERNAL MOBILITY?

Internal mobility refers to the movement of employees within an organization, whether horizontally (changing roles within the same hierarchical level) or vertically (promotions). This practice allows employees to diversify their skills and experiences, increasing their adaptability and personal growth.

BENEFITS OF INTERNAL MOBILITY

1. **Continuous professional development:** Employees have the opportunity to learn new skills and face new challenges, which contributes to their professional growth and satisfaction.
2. **Improved talent retention:** By offering varied career paths within the company, you make employees less likely to look outside for opportunities.
3. **Innovation and creativity:** Exposure to different functions and departments can inspire new ideas and perspectives, enriching organizational creativity and innovation.
4. **Resource optimization:** Internal mobility allows the company to maximize the use of its talents, placing the right people in the right roles at opportune times.

STRATEGIES TO IMPLEMENT INTERNAL MOBILITY

1. **Flexible career paths:** Develop career paths that allow for multiple paths and encourage employees to explore different roles within the company.
2. **Targeted development programs :** Provide specific

training and development that prepares employees for a variety of roles, ensuring they are ready to take advantage of internal opportunities when they arise.
3. **Transparent internal application processes:** Establish a clear and fair system for employees to apply for new positions internally, ensuring everyone has equal access to mobility opportunities.
4. **Performance feedback and assessment:** Use performance assessments to identify potential candidates for internal mobility and discuss their aspirations and career plans.

CHALLENGES OF INTERNAL MOBILITY

Implementing internal mobility can face obstacles, such as resistance from managers who don't want to "lose" their best talent to other parts of the company, or a lack of adequate processes for identifying and preparing employees for new roles. Overcoming these challenges requires an organizational culture that values collective growth and long-term success.

Redefining internal mobility is a crucial strategy for fostering a dynamic and engaged workforce. By enabling employees to explore diverse facets of the organization, you not only enrich their careers, but also strengthen your company's resilience and innovation.

In the next chapter, " **PREVENTING SKILLS OBSOLESCENCE ,**" we'll cover how ongoing employee skills upgrading programs can align them with the company's evolving needs, ensuring your workforce remains competitive and relevant.

PREVENTING SKILLS OBSOLESCENCE

As we explored the importance of internal mobility in the previous chapter, we now turn our attention to a critical issue facing all organizations: skills obsolescence. In this chapter, we'll discuss how continuous upskilling programs can keep your teams aligned with evolving market and technology needs, ensuring your workforce remains competitive and relevant.

UNDERSTANDING SKILLS OBSOLESCENCE

Skills obsolescence occurs when the capabilities that employees possess are no longer relevant due to technological changes, market innovations or changes in industry demands. This phenomenon can lead to a reduction in the company's competitiveness and employee demotivation.

BENEFITS OF CONTINUOUS SKILLS UPDATE

1. **Maintains Competitiveness:** Ensures your company continues to lead in a rapidly changing business environment by adopting the latest technologies and practices.
2. **Employee engagement:** Employees who receive ongoing training feel valued and challenged, which increases job satisfaction and productivity.
3. **Adapting to change:** A workforce that is constantly learning is more adaptable to change, which is crucial in a globalized and volatile market.

STRATEGIES TO IMPLEMENT SKILLS UPDATE

1. **Regular skills assessments:** Conduct regular assessments of employee skills to identify areas in need of development or updating.
2. **Partnerships with educational institutions:** Collaborate with universities, technical institutes and online learning platforms to provide access to relevant courses.
3. **programs :** Develop personalized learning plans that

align with employees' career goals and company needs.
4. **Culture of continuous learning:** Promote an organizational culture that values and encourages continuous learning, offering time and resources for professional development.

CHALLENGES IN PREVENTING SKILLS OBSOLESCENCE

Key challenges include resistance to change from employees, budget limitations for training programs, and difficulty predicting which skills will be most valuable in the future. Overcoming these challenges requires leadership commitment and a clear talent development strategy.

This chapter addressed the critical importance of preventing skill obsolescence through continuous refresher programs. By investing in the ongoing development of your employees, your organization not only maintains its relevance and competitiveness, but also demonstrates a commitment to the growth and well-being of your team.

In the next chapter, " **ORGANIZATIONAL CULTURE AND RETENTION** ", we will explore how a strong organizational culture focused on valuing employees can significantly improve talent retention.

ORGANIZATIONAL CULTURE AND RETENTION

After addressing the importance of keeping employees' skills up to date in the last chapter, let's now explore how a robust organizational culture focused on valuing employees can improve talent retention. This chapter will detail strategies for cultivating a culture that not only attracts but also retains your best talent, transforming your organization into a place where people want to work and stay.

WHAT IS ORGANIZATIONAL CULTURE?

Organizational culture comprises the values, beliefs, understandings and norms shared by members of an organization. It shapes how employees behave among themselves and in relation to work, influencing everything from decision-making to the way challenges are faced.

THE RELATIONSHIP BETWEEN CULTURE AND RETENTION

A positive and engaging organizational culture is one of the most significant factors in employee retention. Cultures that value transparency, mutual respect, inclusion and professional development encourage employees to make a long-term commitment to the organization.

STRATEGIES TO STRENGTHEN CULTURE AND RETENTION

1. **Open communication and honesty:** Promote a culture of openness where feedback is encouraged and valued. This includes both upward and downward communications.
2. **Employee appreciation:** Implement regular recognition programs that celebrate individual and team contributions, showing employees that their work is essential to the company's success.
3. **Growth opportunities:** Provide clear and accessible paths for professional and personal growth within the company, including training, mentoring and promotion possibilities.

4. **Work-life balance :** Offer flexible work policies that help employees balance their personal and professional responsibilities, such as flexible hours and the ability to work remotely.
5. **Engage and empower:** Create an environment where employees feel an integral part of the company's decisions and strategies. This may include participating in planning meetings and working groups for new initiatives.

CHALLENGES IN CULTIVATION OF A POSITIVE CULTURE

Maintaining a positive organizational culture is challenging, especially during periods of significant change such as mergers, acquisitions or restructuring. Resistance to change can be a major obstacle, and discrepancies between announced policies and actual practices can undermine employee confidence.

This chapter discussed how a strong organizational culture focused on valuing employees can be a powerful tool for improving talent retention. By investing in developing a positive culture, your company not only attracts better talent, but also keeps them motivated and committed in the long term.

In the next chapter, " **PERFORMANCE ASSESSMENT TOOLS**", we will explore how effective appraisal systems can help recognize employee progress and commitment, further supporting the retention and development strategies discussed.

PERFORMANCE ASSESSMENT TOOLS

After exploring how several companies have prospered by valuing and retaining internal talent, it is crucial that we address performance assessment tools. This chapter will focus on how to implement effective appraisal systems that not only recognize employee progress and commitment, but also support talent retention and development strategies.

THE IMPORTANCE OF PERFORMANCE EVALUATION

Performance reviews are essential for measuring employee effectiveness and aligning their contributions with the organization's goals. They serve not only as a basis for promotion and compensation decisions, but also as a personal and professional development tool for employees.

ELEMENTS OF AN EFFECTIVE ASSESSMENT TOOL

1. **Objectivity and fairness:** Assessments must be based on clear and objective criteria, established in accordance with the specific functions and contributions expected from employees.
2. **Regular, constructive feedback:** In addition to formal assessments, it is vital to provide ongoing feedback to encourage constant development and adjust behaviors in real time.
3. **Employee participation:** Involve employees in the evaluation process, allowing them to also evaluate their own performance and set personal goals.
4. **360-degree reviews:** Incorporate feedback from multiple sources, including supervisors, peers, and subordinates, for a more complete view of an individual's performance.

STRATEGIES FOR IMPLEMENTATION

1. **Clear definition of goals and expectations:** Ensure all employees understand expectations and evaluation criteria from the start of their roles.

2. **Training for assessors:** Provide adequate training for managers and assessors, ensuring that assessments are carried out fairly and effectively.
3. **Use of technology:** Adopt software-based assessment systems that make it easier to track performance, collect feedback, and analyze data.
4. **Frequent progress reviews:** Establish a regular schedule of reviews, allowing for ongoing adjustments to employee development plans.

CHALLENGES IN PERFORMANCE EVALUATION

Resistance to change from employees or managers can be an obstacle, as can the potential perception of bias in evaluations. Additionally, collecting and analyzing feedback can be challenging without the right tools.

This chapter has highlighted how performance appraisal tools are vital for properly recognizing employees' efforts and aligning their contributions with organizational goals. By implementing robust and transparent evaluation systems, your company can not only improve talent management, but also boost employee motivation and engagement.

In the next chapter, " **BALANCE BETWEEN NEW AND OLD** ", we will discuss how to find the right balance between welcoming new ideas and valuing existing experience and wisdom, ensuring your organization remains dynamic and innovative.

BALANCE BETWEEN NEW AND OLD

In this chapter, we will explore a crucial topic for any organization that seeks innovation without losing the essence of its identity: the balance between the new and the old. This balance is essential to maintain a dynamic and innovative organization, while valuing accumulated experience and wisdom.

THE IMPORTANCE OF BALANCED NEW IDEAS WITH CONSOLIDATED EXPERIENCES

In a rapidly changing business world, it's tempting to focus exclusively on new ideas and technologies. However, established practices and accumulated experience are fundamental to stability and continuity. The real challenge is to integrate the new with the old in a way that maximizes the strengths of both.

STRATEGIES TO ACHIEVE BALANCE

1. **Culture of continuous learning:** Promote a culture where both innovation and tradition are valued. This can be achieved through development programs that encourage employees at all levels to learn and experiment.
2. **Reverse mentoring:** Using reverse mentoring, where younger employees share knowledge about new technologies and trends with more experienced colleagues, can help bring in new perspectives while valuing existing experience.
3. **Diverse innovation committees:** Forming innovation committees with members from different generations and areas of the company can foster a productive dialogue between the "old" and the "new", leading to more balanced solutions.
4. **Pilot projects:** Implement pilot projects that allow you to test new ideas on a small scale before making broad organizational changes. This minimizes risk while enabling innovation.

BENEFITS OF AN EFFECTIVE BALANCE

- **Sustainable innovation :** By balancing new ideas with proven experience, your organization can innovate sustainably and with lower risk.
- **Increased employee engagement:** Providing all employees, regardless of age or experience, the opportunity to contribute and learn can increase engagement and job satisfaction.
- **Continuity and change:** Maintaining a healthy balance helps ensure that change does not come at the expense of losing what has worked well for the organization in the past.

CHALLENGES WHEN NAVIGATING BALANCE

Maintaining the ideal balance can be challenging due to cultural resistance or the difficulty of integrating new technologies harmoniously with legacy systems. Leadership needs to be sensitive and adaptive to manage these tensions.

This chapter has highlighted the importance of maintaining a healthy balance between innovation and tradition within your organization. By doing so, you can enjoy the best of both worlds, ensuring your business remains relevant and competitive in an ever-changing environment.

In the next chapter, " **TRAINING AND DEVELOPMENT** ," we'll explore how to invest in training programs that help long-term employees stay competitive.

TRAINING AND DEVELOPMENT

After discussing the importance of balancing innovation and experience, in this chapter we'll focus on how continued investment in training and development can keep your long-term employees competitive and engaged. This investment not only benefits the individual, but also strengthens the organization as a whole.

THE IMPORTANCE OF CONTINUOUS TRAINING AND DEVELOPMENT

In an ever-evolving job market, ongoing training and development is essential to keep the workforce up to date with the latest skills and knowledge. This commitment to continuous learning demonstrates to employees that the company values their personal and professional growth, which can increase job satisfaction and productivity.

STRATEGIES FOR EFFECTIVE IMPLEMENTATION

1. **Training needs assessment:** Regularly assess the skills and knowledge that are most needed in your organization and identify which employees would benefit most from specific training.
2. **Personalization of training programs:** Tailor training programs to meet individual employee needs, considering their roles, experiences and career goals.
3. **Use of modern technology and methods: Implement e-** learning platforms and utilize training methods that incorporate virtual reality, gamification and mobile learning to make training more accessible and engaging.
4. **Creating career development plans:** Develop career plans that include short- and long-term goals and that are aligned with employees' career aspirations and the company's needs.

BENEFITS OF TRAINING AND DEVELOPMENT

- **Greater employee retention:** Employees who have development opportunities tend to feel more valued and less likely to look for opportunities elsewhere.
- **Improvement in organizational performance:** Well-trained teams work more efficiently and are able to innovate and respond to market challenges more effectively.
- **Learning culture:** A culture that values continuous learning attracts quality talent and encourages a continuous improvement mindset among all employees.

CHALLENGES IN TRAINING AND DEVELOPMENT

Challenges include allocating sufficient budget for comprehensive training programs, measuring the return on investment in such programs, and ensuring that training is relevant and adapted to rapid changes in the industry.

This chapter explored how ongoing training and development is crucial to maintaining a competitive and motivated workforce. Investing in the growth of your employees not only improves organizational effectiveness, but also strengthens employee loyalty and commitment to the company.

In the next chapter, " **SUCCESSION PLANS** ," we will discuss how to prepare experienced employees for leadership positions as part of an effective succession strategy.

SUCCESSION PLANS

After covering the importance of ongoing training and development, in this chapter we will explore how to prepare experienced employees for leadership positions through effective succession plans. These plans are essential to ensure the continuity and stable growth of the organization, in addition to maximizing internal leadership potential.

WHAT ARE SUCCESSION PLANS?

Succession plans are proactive strategies designed to identify and develop future leaders within an organization, ensuring that there are qualified people ready to take on key roles as they become available. These plans are crucial to avoiding critical vacancies and smooth leadership transitions.

THE IMPORTANCE OF SUCCESSION PLANS

Succession plans not only prepare the next generation of leaders, but also strengthen the organizational structure by ensuring that critical knowledge and skills are passed on effectively. They also help mitigate risks associated with the loss of senior leadership due to retirement, job change, or other reasons.

STRATEGIES FOR DEVELOPING EFFECTIVE SUCCESSION PLANS

1. **Talent identification:** Use performance reviews, 360-degree feedback, and other tools to identify employees with leadership potential.
2. **Targeted development:** Provide specific leadership training, mentoring opportunities, and challenging projects that prepare identified candidates for future leadership roles.
3. **Engagement and communication: Keep** succession candidates informed about their potential career paths and engaged in the development process, ensuring they are motivated to advance within the organization.
4. **reviews and adjustments:** Review and adjust the

succession plan regularly to align with changes in company and personnel goals.

BENEFITS OF IMPLEMENTING SUCCESSION PLANS

- **Leadership Continuity:** Ensures a smooth leadership transition that maintains operational and strategic stability.
- **Talent retention:** Encourages talented employees to stay with the company when they see a clear path for advancement.
- **Strong leadership culture:** Promotes a culture where leadership development is prioritized, which can increase morale and organizational performance.

CHALLENGES IN IMPLEMENTING SUCCESSION PLANS

Challenges may include resistance to change, especially from current leaders; difficulties in identifying the right talent; and developing training programs that effectively prepare leaders for future challenges.

Succession plans are an essential tool for any organization that aspires to longevity and continued success. By investing in preparing your future leaders today, you are ensuring your company's growth and stability tomorrow.

In the next chapter, " **ENNCOURAGING INTERNAL INNOVATION** ," we will explore how to foster an environment that not only allows, but encourages employees to innovate and contribute creative ideas that can take the organization to new heights of success.

ENCOURAGING INTERNAL INNOVATION

After exploring how succession plans are fundamental to continuity and leadership development, we now turn to an equally vital force for the sustainable growth of any organization: internal innovation. This chapter will discuss how to foster an environment that not only allows, but actively encourages employees to innovate and contribute creative ideas.

WHAT IS INTERNAL INNOVATION?

Internal innovation refers to the creation of new ideas, products, services and processes within an organization. It is fueled by employees' ability to think creatively and try new approaches in a supportive environment.

THE IMPORTANCE OF INTERNAL INNOVATION

Innovation is the engine of business growth and competitiveness. Organizations that encourage internal innovation can adapt more quickly to market changes, outperform competitors and better meet the needs of their customers.

STRATEGIES TO FOSTER INTERNAL INNOVATION

1. **Culture of openness and experimentation:** Create an organizational culture that celebrates experimentation and accepts failure as part of the innovation process. This encourages employees to take risks and bring new ideas without fear of negative repercussions.
2. **Targeted innovation programs:** Implement specific programs, such as hackathons, internal incubators, or idea competitions, that give employees a platform to innovate and reward the best ideas.
3. **Leadership support:** Ensure leaders at all levels support innovation by providing the resources, time and guidance needed to turn ideas into action.
4. **Tools and resources:** Provide access to tools and technologies that enable innovation, from cutting-edge software to collaborative workspaces that encourage

creative thinking.

BENEFITS OF INTERNAL INNOVATION

- **Adaptation and resilience:** Innovative organizations are better able to adapt to challenges and changes in the market.
- **Talent attraction and retention:** An innovative environment attracts employees who are creative, motivated and committed to continuous improvement.
- **Competitive advantage:** Innovation can lead to unique products and services that differentiate the company in the market.

CHALLENGES IN ENCOURAGING INNOVATION

Some of the key challenges include overcoming organizational inertia, distributing resources between core operations and innovative activities, and measuring the real impact of innovation on business goals.

Encouraging internal innovation is crucial for any organization that aspires to thrive in an ever-changing business environment. By cultivating an environment that values and promotes innovation, your company will not only survive, but thrive, discovering new opportunities and redefining what is possible in your field.

In the next chapter, " **CHANGE MANAGEMENT** ", we will explore how to manage organizational change effectively with the support of experienced employees, easing the transition and ensuring the company remains agile and adaptable in the face of new challenges.

CHANGE MANAGEMENT

After highlighting the importance of encouraging internal innovation in the previous chapter, we will now address a fundamental topic for any organization seeking to adapt and prosper: change management. This chapter will explore effective strategies for managing organizational change, ensuring your company remains agile and adaptable in the face of ongoing challenges.

WHAT IS CHANGE MANAGEMENT?

Change management is a structured process to ensure that changes are implemented smoothly and effectively, minimizing resistance and maximizing benefits. It involves preparing, supporting and helping people to make organizational changes.

THE IMPORTANCE OF CHANGE MANAGEMENT

Organizational changes can include everything from internal restructuring, implementation of new technologies, to changes in business strategy. Effective management is crucial because it helps reduce stress and uncertainty among employees, increases acceptance of change, and improves the implementation of new initiatives.

STRATEGIES FOR EFFECTIVE CHANGE MANAGEMENT

1. **Clear and open communication:** Keep all employees informed about changes, including the why, how and what of the change. Communication must be frequent and transparent.
2. **Employee involvement:** Include employees in the change process, giving them the opportunity to express opinions and contribute ideas. This can increase acceptance and reduce resistance.
3. **Training and support:** Provide adequate training to equip employees with the skills needed to handle new tools or processes. Ongoing support is also crucial to help adapt to the new reality.

4. **Strong leadership :** Have visible and accessible leaders who can guide and inspire confidence during the change process.

BENEFITS OF CHANGE MANAGEMENT

- **Smoother transitions:** Reduces turbulence during periods of change, ensuring operations continue to run without significant disruptions.
- **Greater efficiency and effectiveness:** Increases the likelihood that changes will be implemented effectively and achieve the desired results.
- **Improvement in organizational culture:** Promotes a culture of adaptability and openness, where change is seen as an opportunity rather than a threat.

CHALLENGES IN CHANGE MANAGEMENT

Challenges include overcoming natural resistance to change, communicating effectively at all levels of the organization, and aligning change with existing organizational culture and goals.

Managing change effectively is essential to ensuring your organization not only survives but also thrives in a constantly evolving business environment. By applying the strategies discussed, you can help your business navigate change in a proactive and positive way.

In the next chapter, " **CREATIVE SOLUTIONS TO BUSINESS CHALLENGES** ", we will explore how internal expertise can be used to solve problems creatively and efficiently.

CREATIVE SOLUTIONS TO BUSINESS CHALLENGES

Having explored how to effectively manage change within your organization, we will now turn our attention to how internal experience and skills can be mobilized to creatively and efficiently solve business challenges. This chapter will discuss the importance of leveraging employees' creativity and accumulated knowledge to overcome obstacles and innovate solutions.

THE IMPORTANCE OF CREATIVITY IN BUSINESS

Creativity is a powerful tool in the business environment, essential for innovation and problem solving. It allows companies to find unique solutions to challenges that may seem insurmountable, transforming obstacles into opportunities for growth and differentiation in the market.

STRATEGIES TO FOSTER CREATIVITY

1. **Stimulating environments:** Create workspaces that encourage creative thinking, whether through physical layouts that promote collaboration or through virtual environments that facilitate the exchange of ideas.
2. **Regular brainstorming sessions:** Organize brainstorming sessions where employees can freely express new ideas without initial judgment or restrictions. This can stimulate creative thinking and generate innovative solutions.
3. **Incentives for innovation:** Develop incentive programs that reward employees for ideas that help solve company problems or improve processes.
4. **Team diversity:** Build teams with a diversity of experiences and perspectives. A variety of viewpoints can lead to more creative and comprehensive solutions.

BENEFITS OF CREATIVE SOLUTIONS

- **Effective problem solving:** Creative approaches can lead to more efficient and sustainable solutions to business challenges.

- **Competitive advantage:** Companies that are able to continually innovate stay ahead of the competition.
- **Employee engagement:** Promoting creativity increases job satisfaction as employees feel that their ideas are valued and that they have a real impact on the company.

CHALLENGES IN PROMOTING CREATIVITY

Fostering a truly creative environment can be challenging, especially in business cultures that traditionally value conformity and control. Overcoming these challenges requires a mindset shift in leadership and a willingness to accept risks and experiment.

This chapter has highlighted how cultivating and applying creative solutions to business challenges can not only solve problems effectively but also transform the way your company operates, leading to continuous improvement and innovation. By encouraging creativity among your employees, you are equipping your organization for long-term success in an increasingly competitive market environment.

In the next chapter, " **THE IMPACT OF EMPLOYEE SATISFACTION** ", we will explore how employee satisfaction directly affects company success and how measures to improve well-being at work can contribute to positive business results.

THE IMPACT OF EMPLOYEE SATISFACTION

After exploring how to foster internal creativity and innovation, it's crucial to understand how employee satisfaction directly influences company success. In this chapter, we will discuss the importance of employee well-being and how measures focused on improving job satisfaction can significantly contribute to positive business results.

THE IMPORTANCE OF EMPLOYEE SATISFACTION

Job satisfaction is critical not only to the well-being of employees, but also to the overall health of the organization. Satisfied employees tend to be more productive, loyal and engaged, which reduces turnover and increases operational efficiency.

STRATEGIES TO IMPROVE EMPLOYEE SATISFACTION

1. **Positive work environment:** Create a work environment that promotes mutual respect, collaboration and open communication. A positive environment can significantly improve employee satisfaction.
2. **Recognition and reward:** Develop recognition systems that value employee contributions regularly, not just in annual reviews or promotions.
3. **Growth opportunities:** Provide clear paths for professional and personal growth within the company. Employees who see opportunities to advance are more likely to feel satisfied and committed to the organization.
4. **Work-life balance:** Promote policies that support work-life balance, such as flexible work schedules and telecommuting options.
5. **Feedback and communication:** Keep communication channels open and offer constructive feedback regularly, allowing employees to feel like their voices are heard and valued.

BENEFITS OF EMPLOYEE SATISFACTION

- **productivity** : Satisfied and engaged employees are more productive and efficient in their tasks.
- **Talent retention:** Job satisfaction is a key factor in employee retention, which reduces the costs associated with hiring and training new talent.
- **Improved organizational culture:** A high level of employee satisfaction contributes to a positive organizational culture, which attracts and retains high-quality talent.

CHALLENGES IN IMPROVING EMPLOYEE SATISFACTION

Some of the key challenges include identifying individual employee needs, adjusting organizational policies to support those needs in a sustainable way, and effectively measuring the impact of satisfaction initiatives.

This chapter has highlighted how employee satisfaction is crucial to the success of an organization. Investing in employee well-being not only improves their productivity and loyalty, but also strengthens the company's culture and competitiveness in the market. By implementing the aforementioned strategies, you can ensure that your organization not only meets your employees' expectations, but also exceeds them, resulting in lasting benefits for everyone involved.

In the next chapter, " **CREATING A BUSINESS LEGACY** ," we'll explore how to build a legacy with the help of dedicated, long-time employees.

CREATING A BUSINESS LEGACY

Having covered the importance of employee satisfaction in the previous chapter, let's now explore how you can build a lasting legacy for your company. This chapter will discuss how the contributions of dedicated, long-time employees can be crucial to shaping and perpetuating the values and practices that will define your organization's future.

UNDERSTANDING THE CONCEPT OF BUSINESS LEGACY

A business legacy involves much more than financial success and brand recognition; it's about creating a rich corporate culture that lasts through generations. This includes sustainable practices, business ethics, and a commitment to community and corporate values.

THE IMPORTANCE OF A BUSINESS LEGACY

1. **Continuity:** A strong legacy ensures that the company's vision and values continue to guide its operations and future decisions, even with leadership changes.
2. **Corporate reputation:** Companies with a clear, positive legacy are often seen as more trustworthy and reputable, which can attract quality clients, partners and talent.
3. **Employee motivation:** Knowing they are contributing to something bigger that transcends daily operations can significantly increase employee motivation and engagement.

STRATEGIES FOR BUILDING A BUSINESS LEGACY

1. **Promote and live corporate values:** Ensure company values are clearly communicated, understood and lived at all levels of the organization.
2. **Continued leadership development:** Invest in the development of future leaders who are aligned with the company's culture and values, ensuring the continuity of the legacy.

3. **Commitment to corporate social responsibility:** Getting involved in initiatives that benefit the community and the environment not only helps build a positive legacy, but also strengthens connections with stakeholders.
4. **Documentation and Stories:** Capture and share significant company stories and milestones. This not only helps preserve organizational memory but also inspires future generations to continue the legacy.

CHALLENGES IN CREATING A LEGACY

Maintaining relevance while adhering to traditional values can be challenging, especially in a rapidly changing market. Additionally, ensuring that legacy does not become a set of rigid rules that impede innovation and adaptation is also a delicate balance.

Creating and sustaining a business legacy is an ongoing journey that requires ongoing commitment, vision and dedication from all levels of the organization. By investing in corporate culture, leadership and social responsibility, your company will not only prosper in the present, but also leave a lasting mark that can positively influence future generations.

In the next chapter, " **THE FUTURE OF TALENT MANAGEMENT** ", we will reflect on emerging trends and how companies can adapt to continue valuing and retaining talent effectively.

THE FUTURE OF TALENT MANAGEMENT

We have reached the end of our exploratory journey on how to value and retain talent in the modern corporate landscape. This final chapter will reflect on emerging trends in talent management and discuss how companies can adapt to meet future challenges while continuing to value and retain talent effectively.

EMERGING TRENDS IN TALENT MANAGEMENT

1. **Digitization and automation:** Technology will continue to play a crucial role in talent management, offering new tools for recruitment, training and development. Automation can free up human talent to focus on more strategic and creative tasks.
2. **Remote work and flexibility:** The COVID-19 pandemic has accelerated the adoption of remote work, a trend that is likely to persist. Companies will need to find ways to manage and engage globally distributed teams while maintaining corporate culture and collaboration.
3. **Emphasis on diversity and inclusion:** There will be an increasing focus on creating more inclusive and diverse workplaces. Diversity is not just an issue of equity; it is also a competitive advantage that promotes innovation and market understanding.
4. **Continuous development and learning:** With the rapid pace of technological change, continuous learning will be essential. Companies will have to invest in learning and development opportunities to keep their teams up to date with the latest skills and knowledge.

ADAPTATION TO CHANGES IN TALENT MANAGEMENT

1. **Adopt innovative technologies:** Utilize online learning platforms, performance management software, and digital communications tools to keep teams engaged and productive.
2. **Promote work flexibility:** Offer options such as flexible

schedules, compressed workweeks and remote work to attract and retain talent, especially among younger generations who value work-life balance.
3. **Strengthen inclusion strategies:** Implement policies that promote equal opportunities for all employees, regardless of their age, gender, ethnicity or origin, ensuring that everyone feels valued and able to contribute fully.
4. **Foster a culture of learning and innovation:** Encourage a culture that values curiosity, experimentation and continuous learning to help the organization adapt and thrive in an ever-changing environment.

As we look to the future, it is clear that talent management will continue to be a dynamic and challenging area. Organizations that quickly adapt to change, value their employees and invest in their development will be better positioned to achieve success in the 21st century business landscape. We hope the strategies and insights shared in this book inspire you to transform your approach to talent management and build an organization that not only survives, but thrives in the decades to come.

Thank you for joining us on this in-depth journey through the world of talent management. Good luck applying these concepts and strategies to your own organization, and may you build a bright and lasting future for your company and the talents that comprise it.

As we turn the final page of this journey together, I sincerely hope that the learnings shared here have touched your heart and sparked new perspectives. If this book has brought you any value, I kindly ask that you take a few moments to leave a review on Amazon. Your words not only help me grow and hone my craft, but they also guide other readers in their quests for knowledge and inspiration. Your opinion is a valuable gift, both for me and for the community of readers looking for stories that transform. I sincerely thank you for sharing this journey with me and I hope we can meet again in the pages of a new adventure.

REGINALDO OSNILDO

Hello, I'm Reginaldo Osnildo, author and innovator in the areas of sales, technology, and communication strategies. My experience ranges from the academic environment, as a professor and researcher at the University of Southern Santa Catarina, to practice as a strategist at Grupo Catarinense de Rádios. With a PhD in sales narratives and digital convergence, and a master's degree in storytelling and social imaginary, I bring my readers a unique fusion of theory and practice. My goal is to provide knowledge in a simple, practical and didactic language, encouraging direct application in personal and professional life.

Yours sincerely

Reginaldo Osnildo

+55 48 991913865

reginaldoosnildo@gmail.com

www.ingramcontent.com/pod-product-compliance
Lightning Source LLC
Chambersburg PA
CBHW070355230526
45471CB00006B/2582